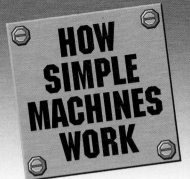

HOW
SIMPLE
MACHINES
WORK

HOW RAMPS, WEDGES, AND SCREWS WORK

by **Jim Mezzanotte**

Reading consultant: Susan Nations, M.Ed.,
author/literacy coach/consultant

Science and curriculum consultant: Debra Voege, M.A.,
science and math curriculum resource teacher

WEEKLY READER®
PUBLISHING

Please visit our web site at: www.garethstevens.com
For a free color catalog describing our list of high-quality books,
call 1-800-542-2595 (USA) or 1-800-387-3178 (Canada).
Our fax: 1-877-542-2596

Library of Congress Cataloging-in-Publication Data

Mezzanotte, Jim.
   How ramps, wedges, and screws work / by Jim Mezzanotte.
     p. cm. — (How simple machines work)
   Includes bibliographical references and index.
   ISBN-10: 0-8368-7349-1 — ISBN-13: 978-0-8368-7349-8 (lib. bdg.)
   ISBN-10: 0-8368-7354-8 — ISBN-13: 978-0-8368-7354-2 (softcover)
   1. Inclined planes—Juvenile literature. I. Title. II. Series: Mezzanotte, Jim.
   How simple machines work.
   TJ147.M493   2006
   621.8—dc22   2006008669

This edition first published in 2007 by
Weekly Reader® Books
An Imprint of Gareth Stevens Publishing
1 Reader's Digest Rd.
Pleasantville, NY 10570-7000 USA

Managing editor: Mark J. Sachner
Art direction: Tammy West
Cover design, page layout, and illustrations: Dave Kowalski
Photo research: Sabrina Crewe

Picture credits: Cover, title, © Tom & Dee Ann McCarthy/CORBIS; p. 5 © Neil Beer/CORBIS; p.
6 © Jim Sugar/CORBIS; p. 7 © Chris Fairclough/Chris Fairclough Worldwide; p. 11
© Jose Luis Pelaez, Inc./CORBIS; p. 15 © David Young-Wolff/PhotoEdit; p. 16
© Annebicque Bernard/CORBIS SYGMA; pp. 18, 19 © David Frazier/Photo Edit; p. 20
© Randy Faris/CORBIS; p. 21 © Michael Newman/PhotoEdit

Printed in the United States of America

3 4 5 6 7 8 9 10 09 08

TABLE OF CONTENTS

Chapter One: The World of Inclined Planes 4

Chapter Two: How Ramps and Wedges Work.........8

Chapter Three: How Screws Work 12

Chapter Four: Jobs for Inclined Planes.................17

Glossary..22

For More Information..23

Index 24

Cover and title page: Ramps help people move things more easily. This slide is a ramp that helps children move themselves along with almost no effort at all!

CHAPTER 1

THE WORLD OF INCLINED PLANES

Do you know what a plane is? No, not the kind that flies! A plane can also be any flat surface. An **inclined plane** is one that is slanted at an angle, like a hill.

Ramps, wedges, and screws are all inclined planes. They help people do different jobs. A ramp lets people move things more easily. A wedge can split things apart. Screws fasten things together.

This road is a ramp. Cars travel uphill on it gradually. Traveling this way takes less work.

A knife is a wedge. It cuts this onion by splitting it apart.

Inclined planes come in different forms. A staircase, for example, is a ramp. So is a slide at a theme park. Knives and scissors have wedges for cutting.

When you tighten the cap on a bottle, you are using an inclined plane. The screw-on top has a ramp on it.

The screw-on top to this bottle uses a ramp to help get it on and off.

CHAPTER

HOW RAMPS AND WEDGES WORK

Imagine you must put a heavy box into a truck. The box is a **load**. The truck is high off the ground. It is hard to lift the box that high.

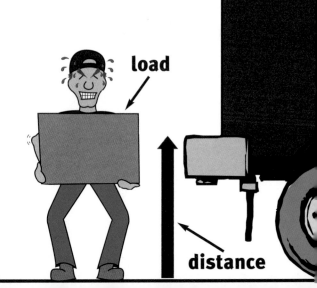

load

distance

So you find a long board. One end rests on the truck. The other end rests on the ground. The board is now a ramp. Using the ramp, you raise the box a little at a time. The box travels farther than if you lifted it straight up. But lifting it is much easier. You use less **effort** over a longer distance.

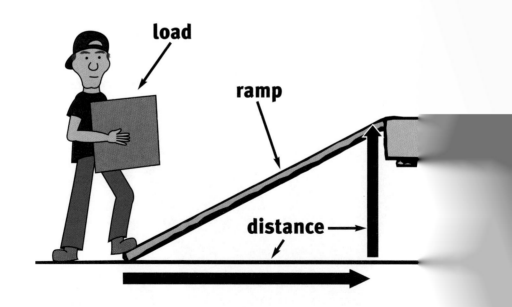

load

ramp

distance

A wedge is two inclined planes. It can help split things. An axe is a wedge. It can split a log. As the axe goes in, the two inclined planes create a sideways force. They push apart the log. The axe must go far into the log to split it just a little bit. But the swinging effort is small compared to the axe's splitting power.

effort

sideways force

wedge

sideways force

The blades on these scissors are wedges. They cut the paper by splitting it.

Knifes and scissors work just like axes. Their blades are shaped like wedges. As the sharp edge goes into the thing you cut, the wedge splits it apart.

CHAPTER 3

HOW SCREWS WORK

Inclined planes are at work in screws, too. A screw has ridges, called threads. The threads are really one long ramp that **spirals** around the screw.

Screws keep things together. Imagine you want to join two boards placed one over the other. You start to put a screw into the top board. As you turn the screw, the threads create grooves. The threads move in these grooves. As you keep turning, the threads pull the screw down into both boards. The boards get pulled tightly together.

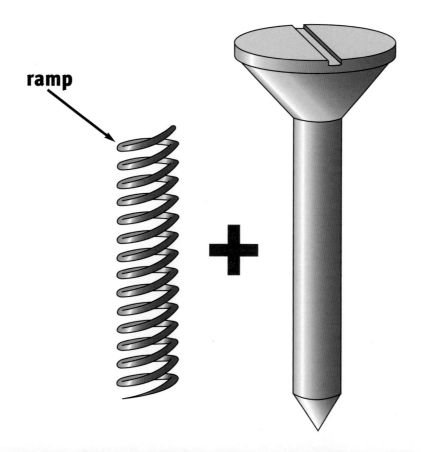

ramp

It usually takes many turns to get the screw in. The threads are a long ramp. They add distance to the effort because they spiral around and around the screw. With just a little turning effort, however, you get a lot of pulling force. Again, you use less effort over a longer distance.

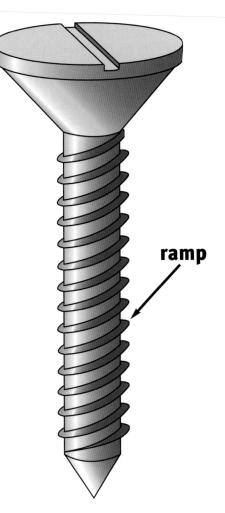

ramp

There are other kinds of screws. A bottle cap has grooves that match threads on the bottle. A drill bit is also a kind of screw. It can make a hole in something, such as wood. As the tip cuts through the wood, the rest of the drill bit pulls the wood out.

This drill is a kind of screw. As it spins, it makes a hole in the wood.

Like ramps and wedges, screws are **simple machines**. They help you do a lot of work without a lot of effort. In this case, "work" just means moving something. Even a light bulb screwed into a **socket** is a simple machine! Today, a lot of machines are complicated. But they are often many simple machines working together.

The end of a lightbulb is also a screw. Screws and other simple machines help us in many ways.

CHAPTER 4

JOBS FOR INCLINED PLANES

People have used inclined planes for thousands of years. Early hunters used wedge-shaped stones for cutting. Ancient Egyptians may have used ramps. They built huge **pyramids** out of stone blocks. Using ramps, they could have dragged the blocks to a great height.

Long ago, a Greek man learned how simple machines work. His name was Archimedes. He invented **Archimedes' screw**. This screw fits inside a tube. It can raise water from a low place to a high place. When the screw turns, it lifts water up through the tube by pulling water along its threaded surface. It can raise other things, such as grain and flour. It even raises wet cement out of a cement truck!

Archimedes' screw

Archimedes' screw raises wet cement out of this truck. As the inside of the truck turns, the screw pulls the cement up its threaded surface.

This plane's propeller is a screw. It pulls the plane through the air.

A **propeller** is also a kind of screw. Propellers pull air through them. This action forces the plane forward through the air.

Does your jacket have a zipper? The zipper has two separate rows of "teeth." When you pull down the zipper, a wedge forces the teeth apart.

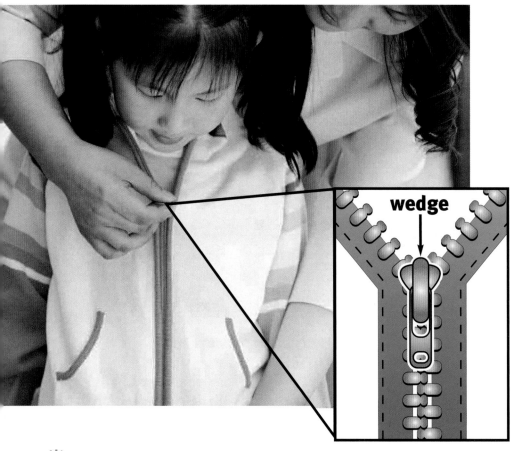

wedge

A zipper works by using a wedge.

A ramp helps these people go up and down between levels of a building.

Today, inclined planes help with many other jobs, too. Some jobs are big, and some are small. Can you think of any other jobs for inclined planes?

GLOSSARY

Archimedes' screw: a device that can draw water from a low place to a high place. It is a kind of screw inside a tube. When the bottom end of the tube goes into water, turning the screw makes water come out the top end. It can be used to raise up different liquids and powders.

effort: the force, or action, that you use to move something

inclined planes: flat surfaces that are on a slant, like a hill. Inclined planes make it easier to move things, split things, or hold things together. They include ramps, wedges, and screws.

load: anything that you move or change. A load can be a box that you lift or a log that needs splitting. It can also be the wood that a screw must enter.

propeller: a spinning device that has wide blades. Like other screws, propellers can pull on things. A plane's propeller pulls on the air, pulling the plane forward. A boat's propeller pushes it by pulling the water from behind.

pyramids: tall structures built by ancient people in Egypt and other places. The base of a pyramid is a square. Its four sides all slant toward each other to form a point on top.

simple machines: devices with few or no moving parts. They let you do a lot of work without a lot of effort.

socket: an opening or a hole that forms a holder into which you may put something

spirals: winds around in a tight circle

FOR MORE INFORMATION

BOOKS

Inclined Planes and Wedges. Early Bird Physics (series). Sally M. Walker and Roseann Feldmann (Lerner Publications)

Ramps and Wedges. Useful Machines (series). Chris Oxlade (Heinemann)

WEB SITES

Edheads: Simple Machines
edheads.org/activities/simple-machines/
At this interactive site, you can learn all about simple machines, including pulleys.

Mikids.com: Simple Machines
www.mikids.com/Smachines.htm
This site has examples of simple machines, including pulleys. It also has fun activities to help you learn more about simple machines.

Publisher's note to educators and parents: Our editors have carefully reviewed these Web sites to ensure that they are suitable for children. Many Web sites change frequently, however, and we cannot guarantee that a site's future contents will continue to meet our high standards of quality and educational value. Be advised that children should be closely supervised whenever they access the Internet.

INDEX

airplanes 19

axes 10

boats 19

bottle caps 7, 15

cement 18

drills 15

Egyptians 17

hills 4, 5

knives 6, 11

lightbulbs 16

scissors 6, 11

staircases 6

threads 12, 13

work 5, 16

zippers 20

About the Author

Jim Mezzanotte has written many books for children. He lives in Milwaukee with his wife and two sons. He uses simple machines every day.